THE TRIALS OF
RODERICK SPODE
THE HUMAN
ANT
BY DAVID MAMET

sourcebooks

Cover design by Charles Brock/FaceOut Studio
Cover illustrations by David Mamet

Published by Sourcebooks, Inc.
P.O. Box 4410, Naperville, Illinois 60567-4410
(630) 961-3900
Fax: (630) 961-2168
www.sourcebooks.com

Library of Congress Cataloging-in-Publication Data

Mamet, David.
The trials of Roderick Spode "The human ant" / David Mamet.
p. cm.
1. Graphic novels. I. Title.
PN6727.M2347T75 2010
741.5'973--dc22

2010000662

Printed and bound in the United States of America.
BG 10 9 8 7 6 5 4 3 2 1

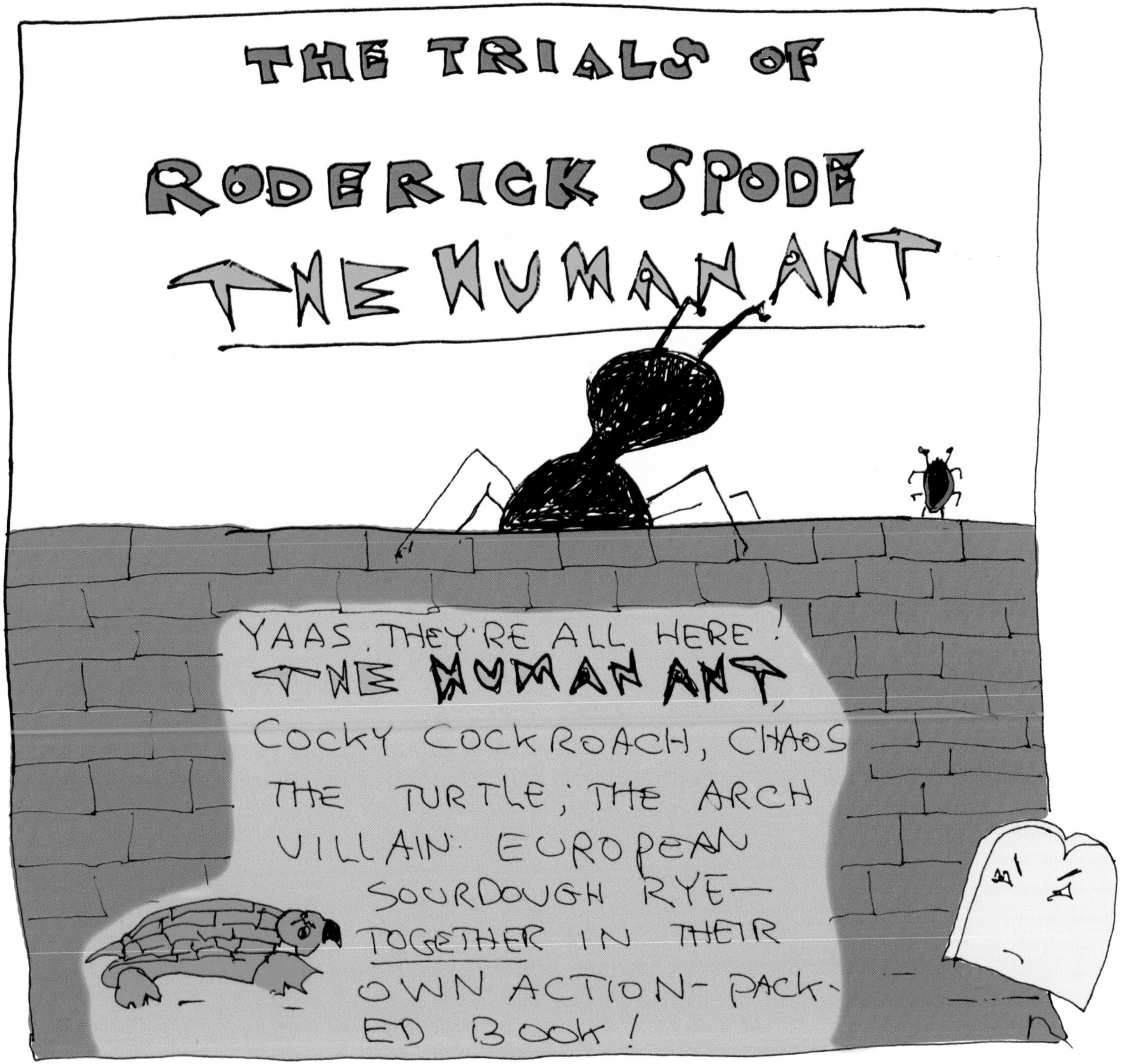
THE TRIALS OF
RODERICK SPODE
THE HUMAN ANT
YAAS, THEY'RE ALL HERE! THE HUMAN ANT, COCKY COCKROACH, CHAOS THE TURTLE; THE ARCH VILLAIN: EUROPEAN SOURDOUGH RYE— TOGETHER IN THEIR OWN ACTION-PACKED BOOK!

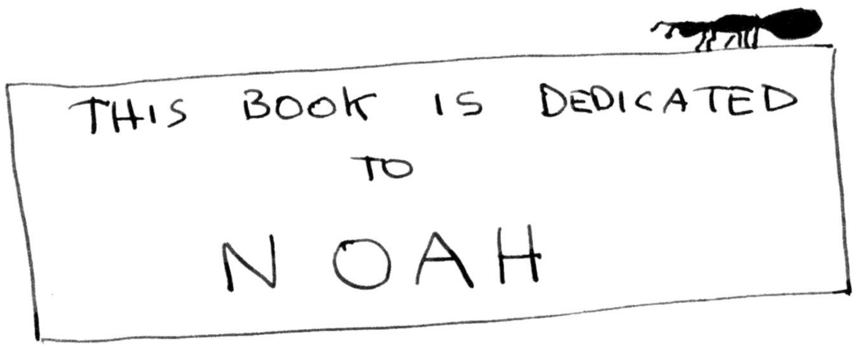
THIS BOOK IS DEDICATED
TO
NOAH

O, SMILE, YE SACRED
NINE
UPON THIS POOR
RETELLING OF THE
MOST HUMAN OF
FANTASIES-
THE ANCIENT TALE OF
MAN
TURNED INTO
ANT

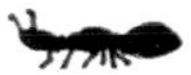

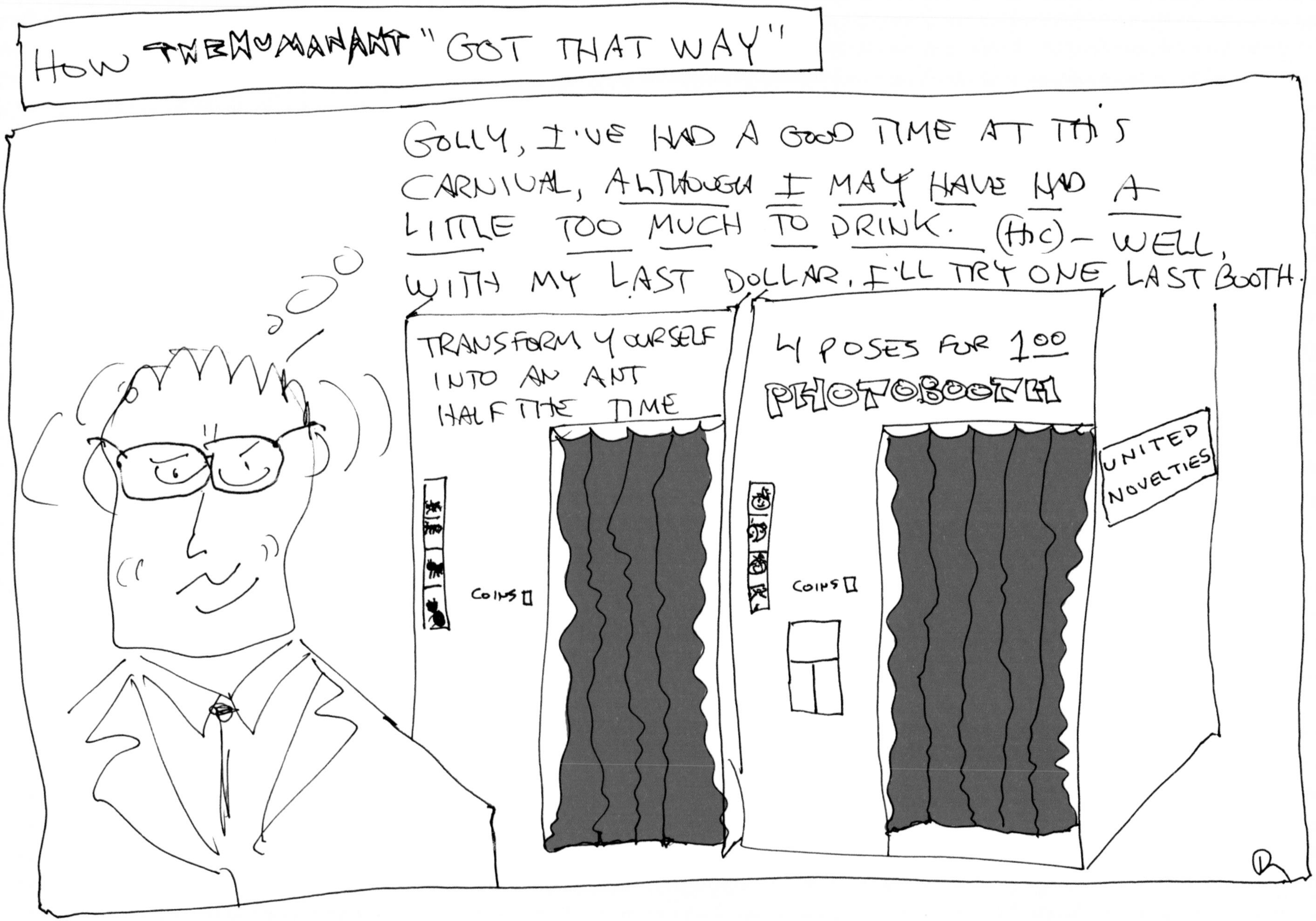
HOW THE HUMAN ANT "GOT THAT WAY"
GOLLY, I'VE HAD A GOOD TIME AT THIS CARNIVAL, ALTHOUGH I MAY HAVE HAD A LITTLE TOO MUCH TO DRINK. (HIC) – WELL, WITH MY LAST DOLLAR, I'LL TRY ONE LAST BOOTH.
TRANSFORM YOURSELF INTO AN ANT HALF THE TIME
COINS
4 POSES FOR 1.00
PHOTOBOOTH
COINS
UNITED NOVELTIES

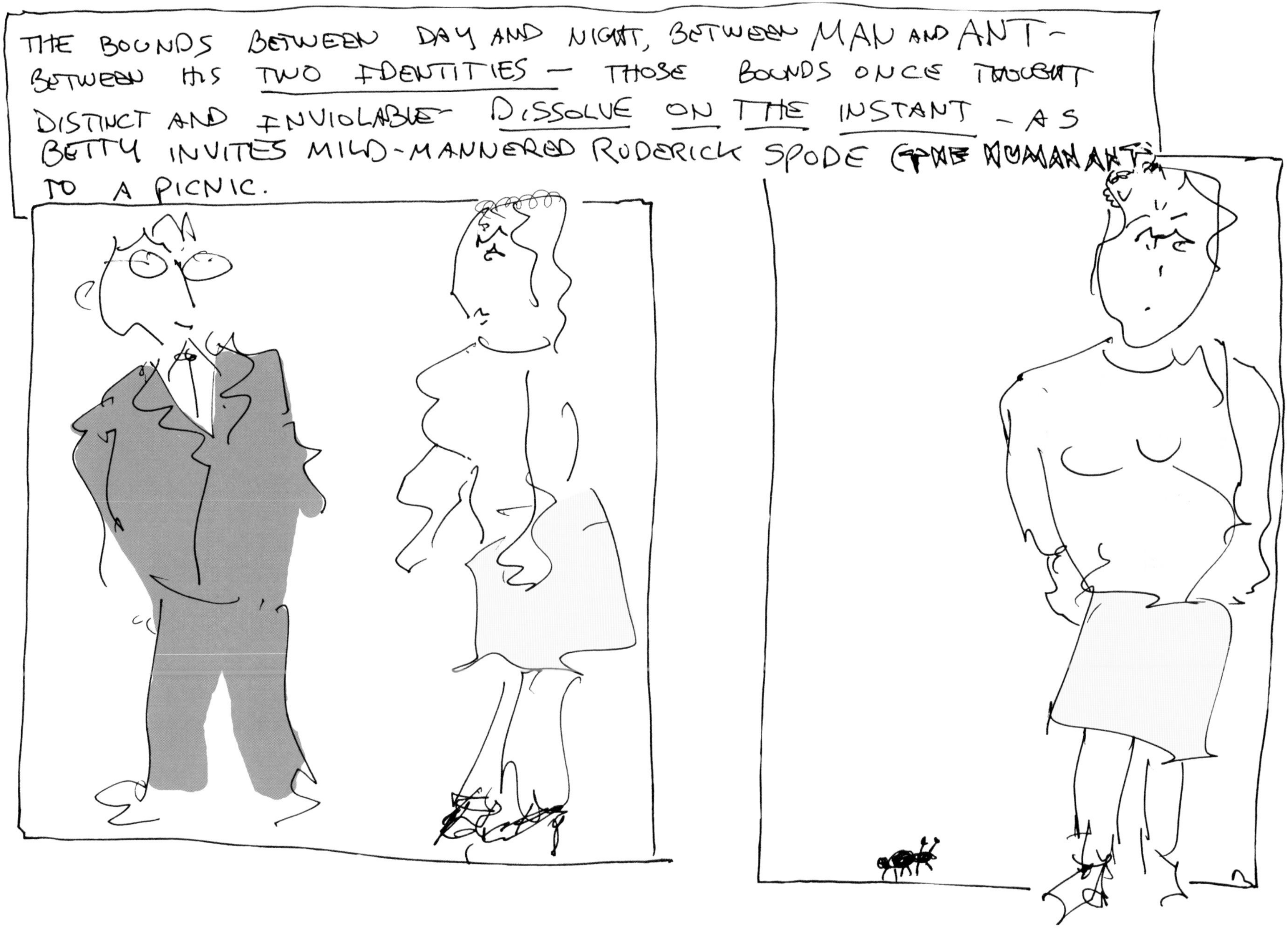
THE BOUNDS BETWEEN DAY AND NIGHT, BETWEEN MAN AND ANT – BETWEEN HIS TWO IDENTITIES – THOSE BOUNDS ONCE THOUGHT DISTINCT AND INVIOLABLE DISSOLVE ON THE INSTANT – AS BETTY INVITES MILD-MANNERED RODERICK SPODE (THE HUMAN ANT) TO A PICNIC.

AN UNFORTUNATE DELAY

POLICE COMMISSIONER FLAGSTONE BROADCASTS THE ANTSIGNAL SUMMONING T.M.A. TO HEADQUARTERS - A SIGNAL THE MIGHTY MIDGET (THROUGH NO FAULT OF HIS OWN) DOES NOT RECEIVE. THE COMMISSIONER, UNAWARE OF THE MISCOMMUNICATION, SPENDS IRREPLACEABLE MINUTES EXPLAINING THE FACTS OF THE CASE TO A BREADCRUMB.

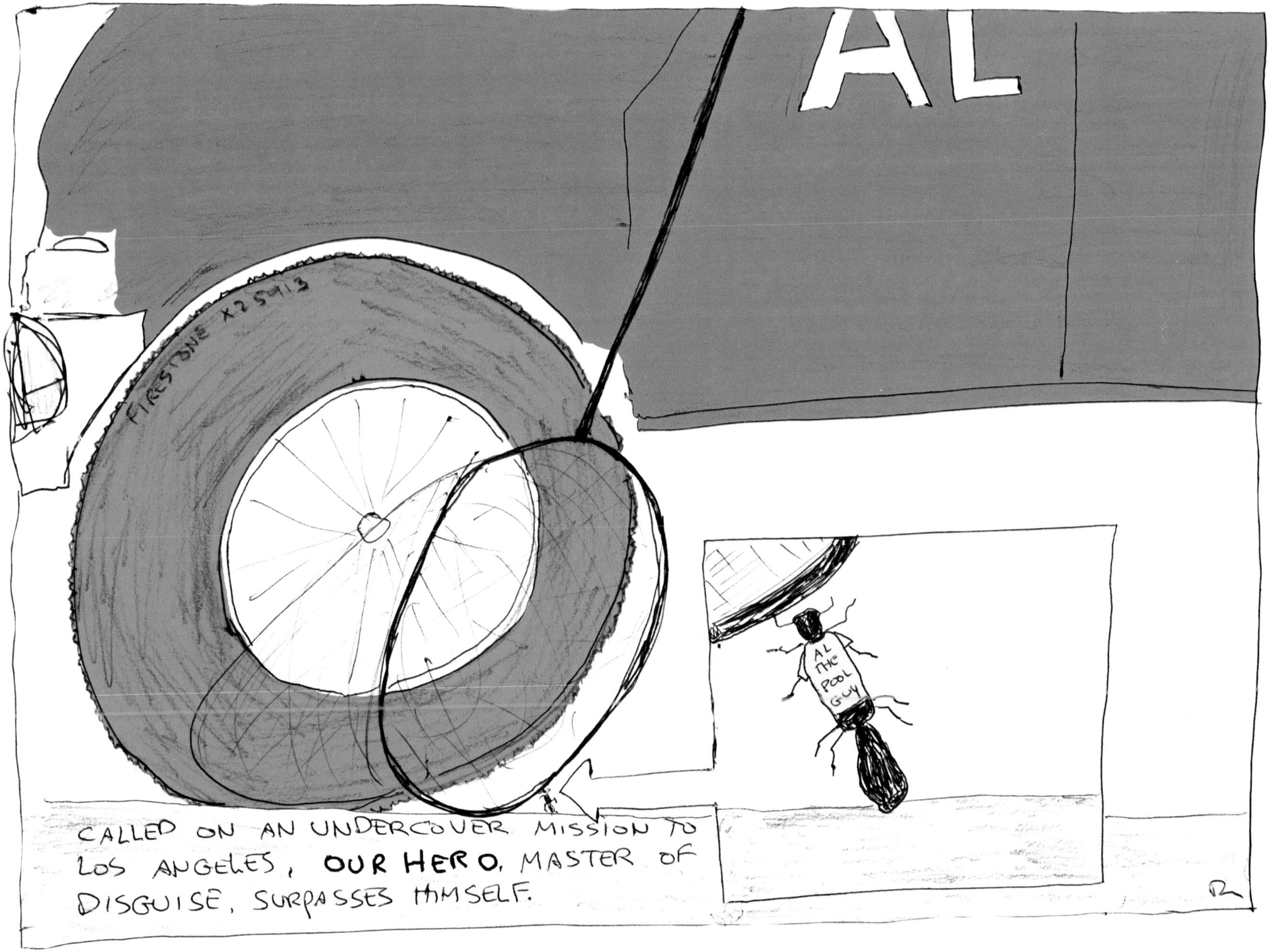
AL
FIRESTONE X25913
AL THE POOL GUY
CALLED ON AN UNDERCOVER MISSION TO LOS ANGELES, **OUR HERO**, MASTER OF DISGUISE, SURPASSES HIMSELF.

UNDERCOVER AS "AL, THE POOL GUY",
T̶H̶E̶ ̶H̶U̶M̶A̶N̶ ̶A̶N̶T̶ IS INVITED OUT FOR DRINKS BY
ELAINE WETHERBY, ONE OF HIS "CLIENTS", AND A
PRIME SUSPECT IN THE CASE. HE SHOPS FOR
CLOTHING APPROPRIATE TO THE LOCALE AND THE
CIRCUMSTANCES.

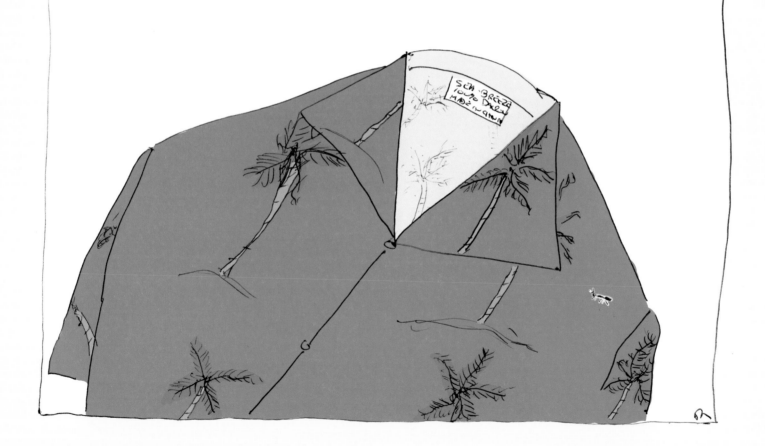

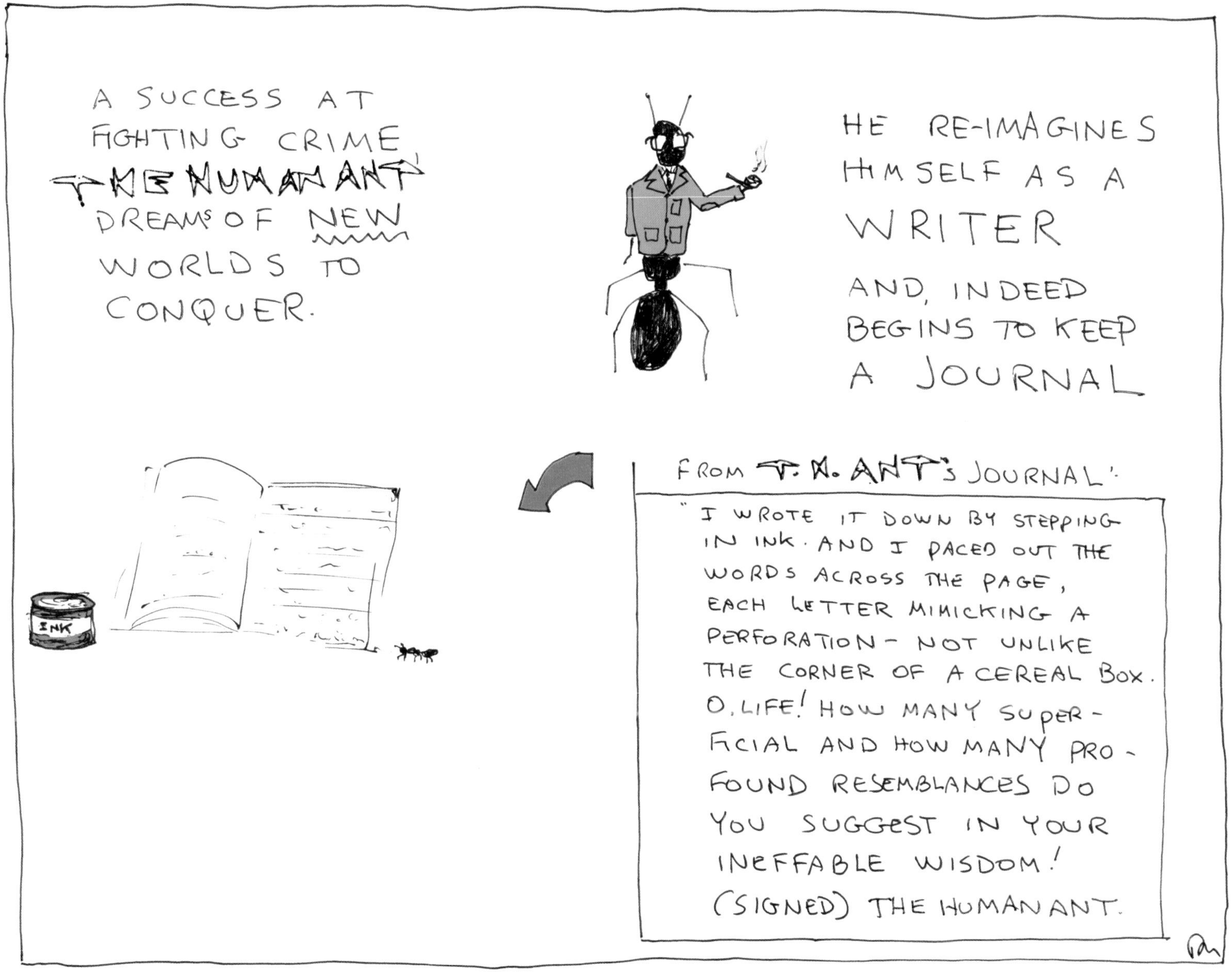
A SUCCESS AT FIGHTING CRIME, THE HUMAN ANT DREAMS OF NEW WORLDS TO CONQUER.
HE RE-IMAGINES HIMSELF AS A WRITER
AND, INDEED BEGINS TO KEEP A JOURNAL
FROM T. H. ANT's JOURNAL:
"I WROTE IT DOWN BY STEPPING IN INK. AND I PACED OUT THE WORDS ACROSS THE PAGE, EACH LETTER MIMICKING A PERFORATION - NOT UNLIKE THE CORNER OF A CEREAL BOX. O, LIFE! HOW MANY SUPER-FICIAL AND HOW MANY PRO-FOUND RESEMBLANCES DO YOU SUGGEST IN YOUR INEFFABLE WISDOM! (SIGNED) THE HUMAN ANT.
INK

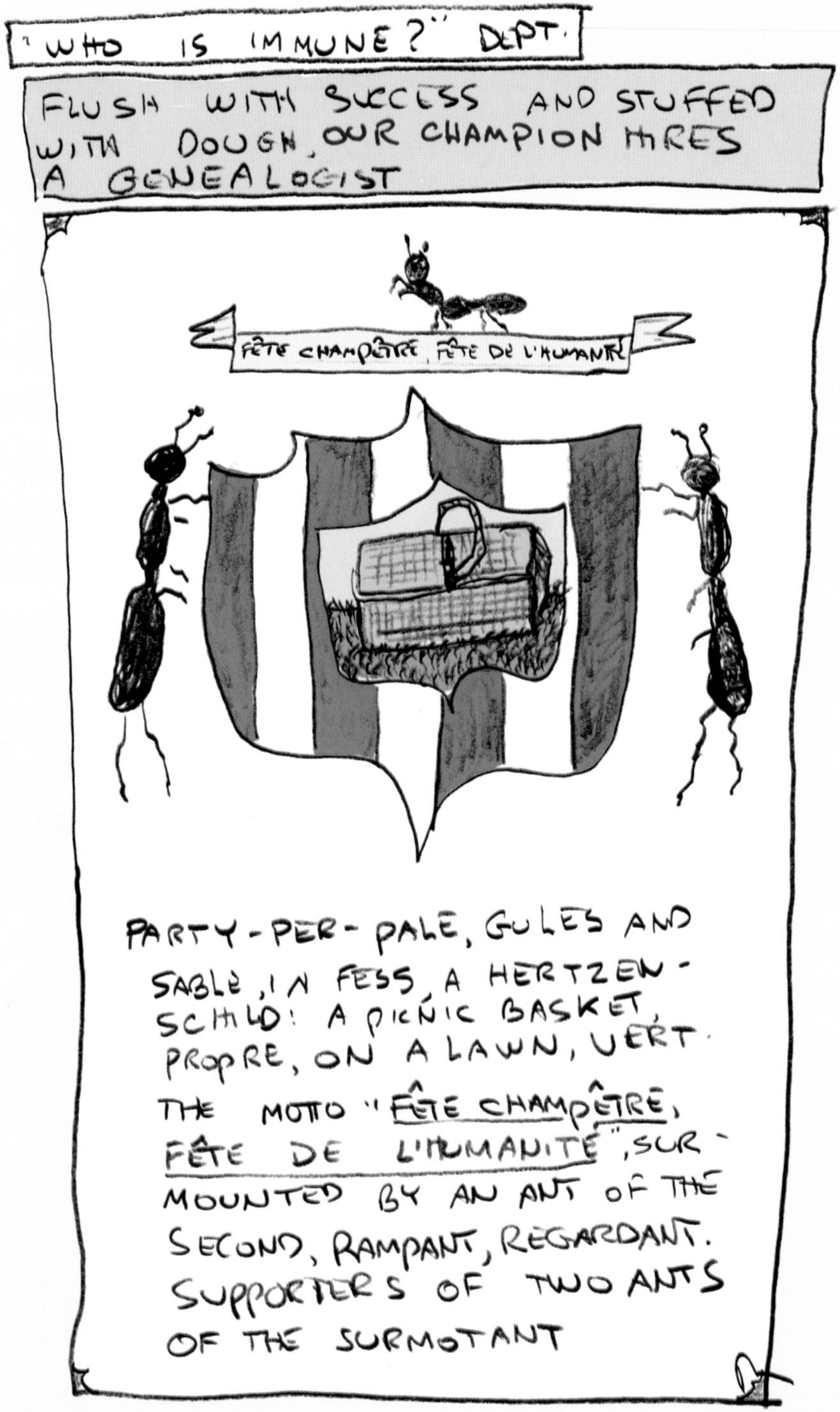
"WHO IS IMMUNE?" DEPT.
FLUSH WITH SUCCESS AND STUFFED WITH DOUGH, OUR CHAMPION HIRES A GENEALOGIST
FÊTE CHAMPÊTRE, FÊTE DE L'HUMANITÉ
PARTY-PER-PALE, GULES AND SABLE, IN FESS A HERTZEN-SCHILD: A PICNIC BASKET, PROPRE, ON A LAWN, VERT. THE MOTTO "FÊTE CHAMPÊTRE, FÊTE DE L'HUMANITÉ", SURMOUNTED BY AN ANT OF THE SECOND, RAMPANT, REGARDANT. SUPPORTERS OF TWO ANTS OF THE SURMOTANT

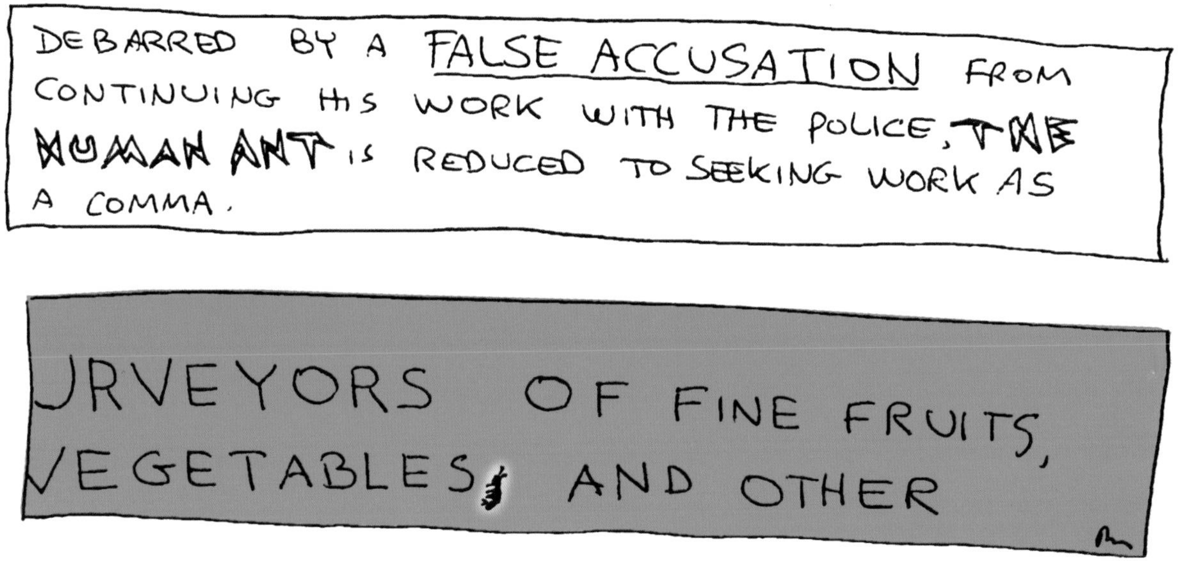
DEBARRED BY A FALSE ACCUSATION FROM CONTINUING HIS WORK WITH THE POLICE, THE HUMAN ANT IS REDUCED TO SEEKING WORK AS A COMMA.
URVEYORS OF FINE FRUITS,
VEGETABLES AND OTHER

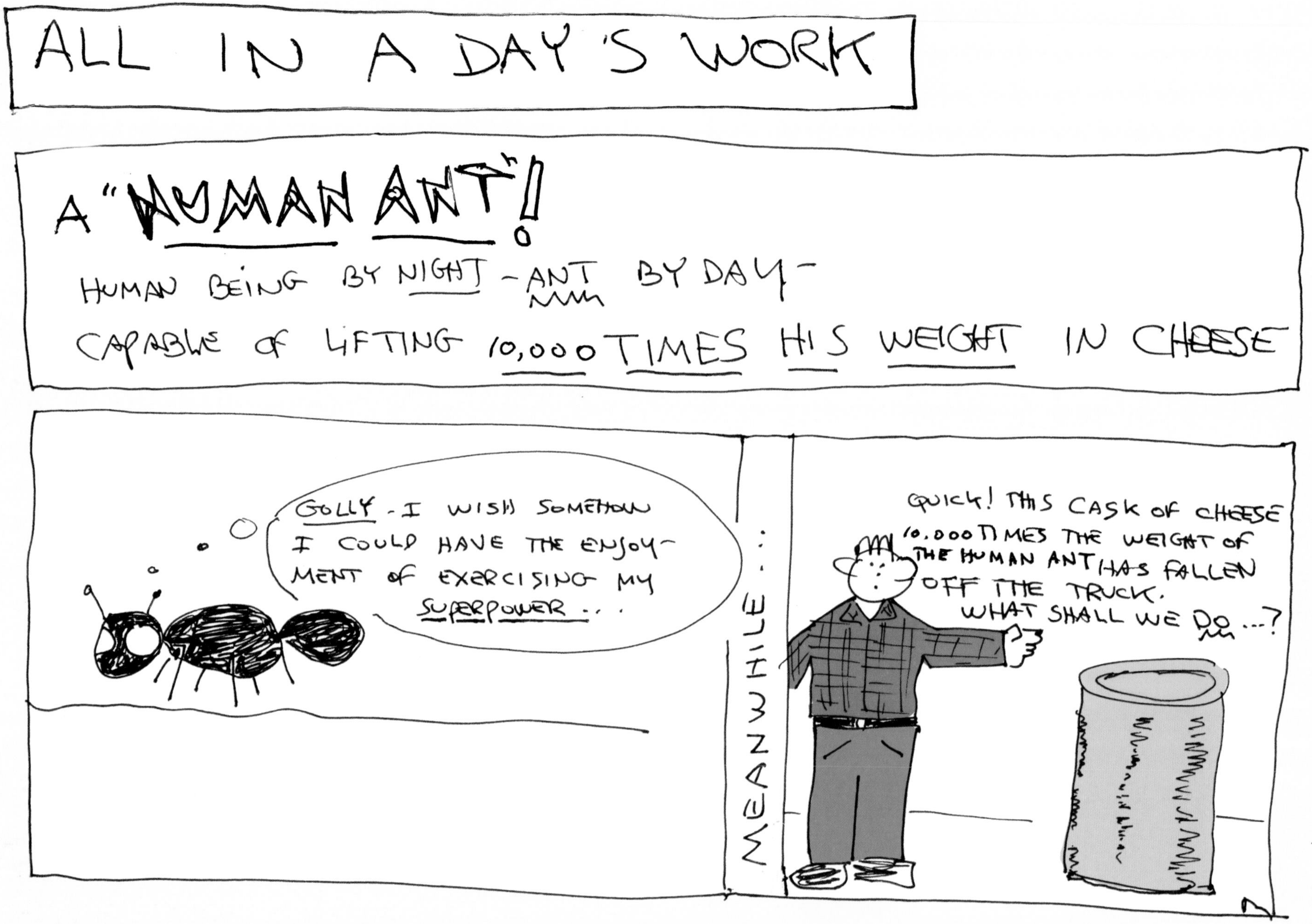
ALL IN A DAY'S WORK
A "HUMAN ANT"!
HUMAN BEING BY NIGHT - ANT BY DAY -
CAPABLE OF LIFTING 10,000 TIMES HIS WEIGHT IN CHEESE
GOLLY - I WISH SOMEHOW I COULD HAVE THE ENJOYMENT OF EXERCISING MY SUPERPOWER . . .
MEANWHILE . . .
QUICK! THIS CASK OF CHEESE 10,000 TIMES THE WEIGHT OF THE HUMAN ANT HAS FALLEN OFF THE TRUCK. WHAT SHALL WE DO . . .?

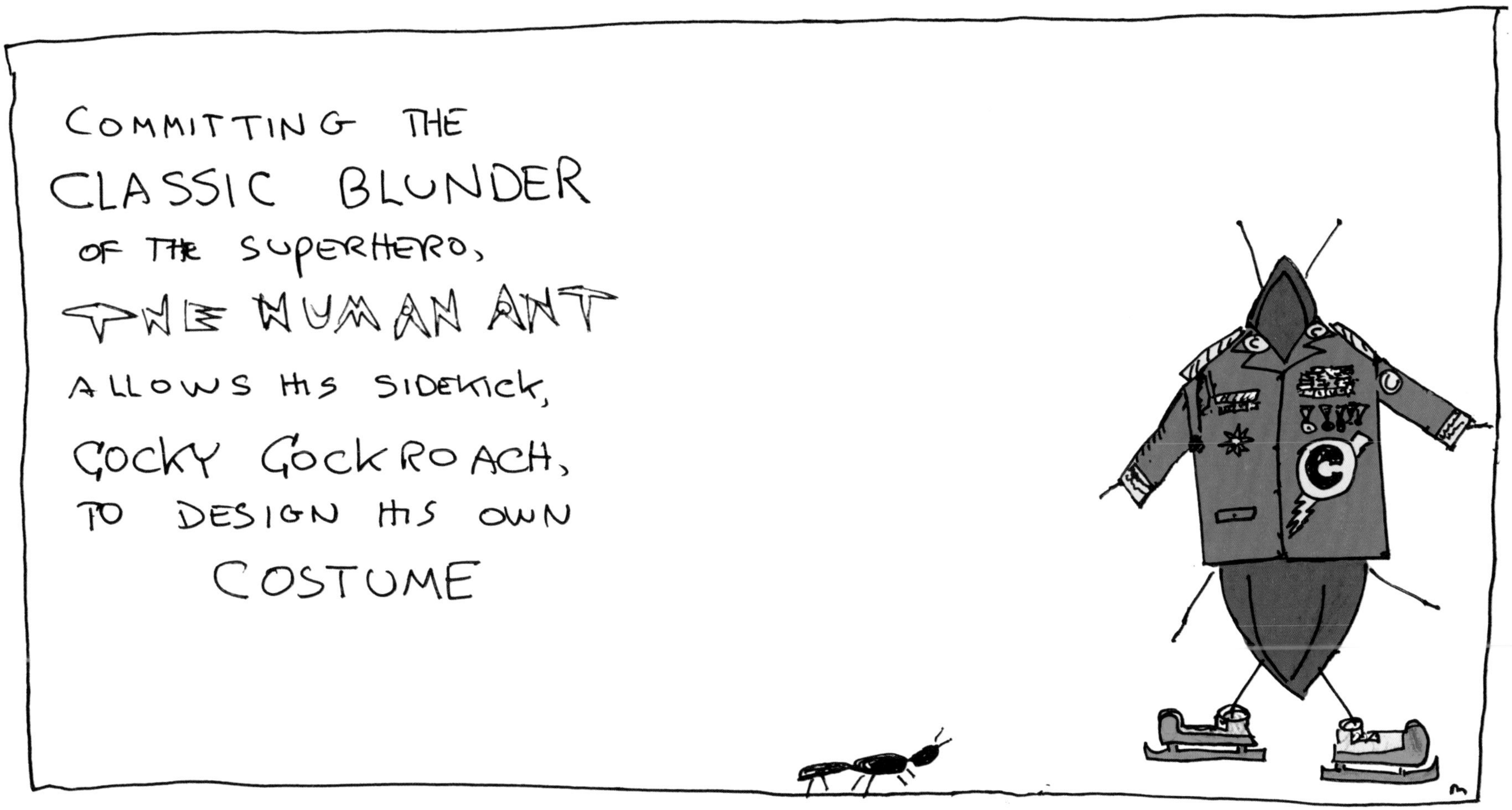
COMMITTING THE
CLASSIC BLUNDER
OF THE SUPERHERO,
THE HUMAN ANT
ALLOWS HIS SIDEKICK,
COCKY COCKROACH,
TO DESIGN HIS OWN
COSTUME

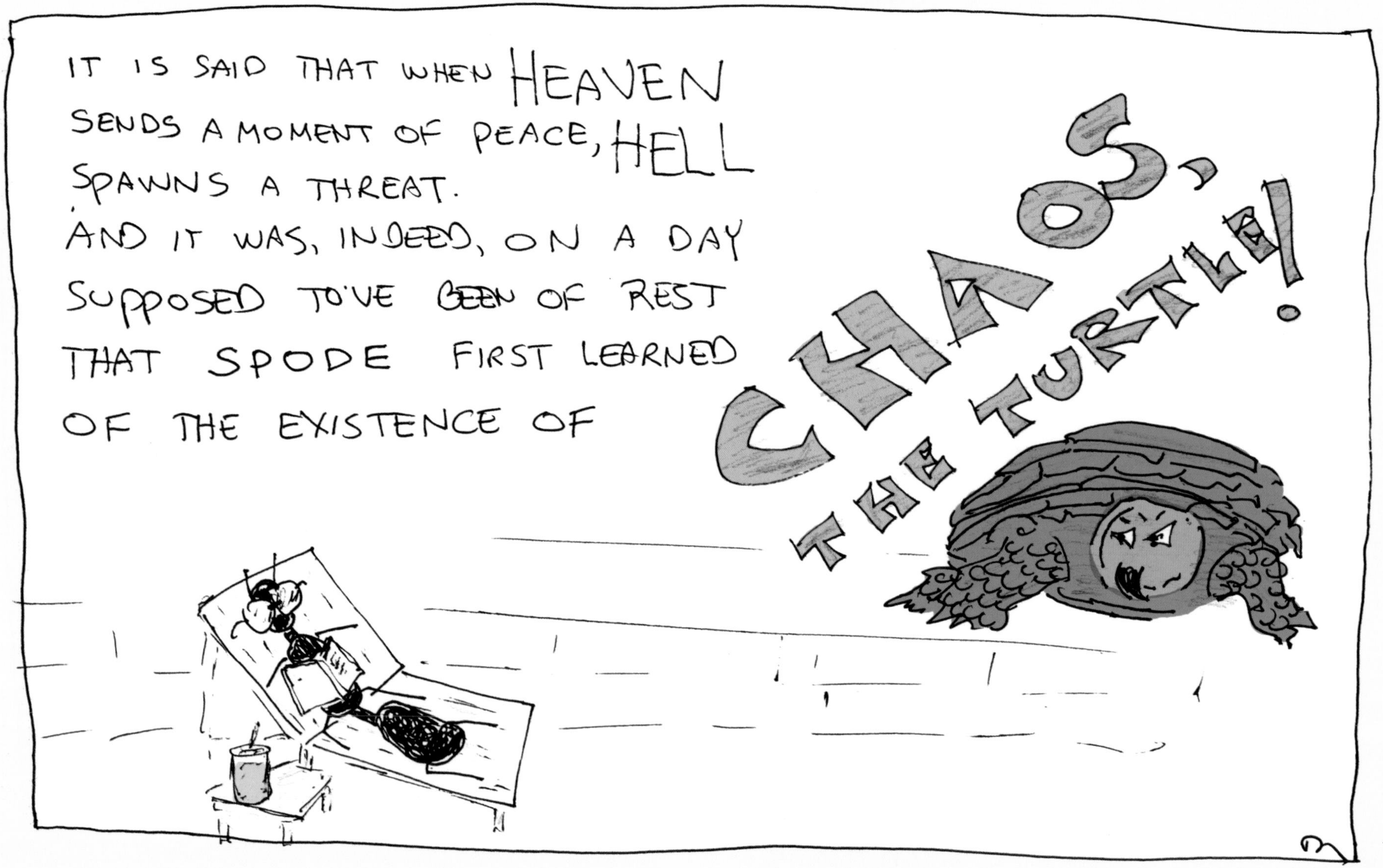
IT IS SAID THAT WHEN HEAVEN SENDS A MOMENT OF PEACE, HELL SPAWNS A THREAT.
AND IT WAS, INDEED, ON A DAY SUPPOSED TO'VE BEEN OF REST THAT SPODE FIRST LEARNED OF THE EXISTENCE OF
CHAOS, THE TURTLE!

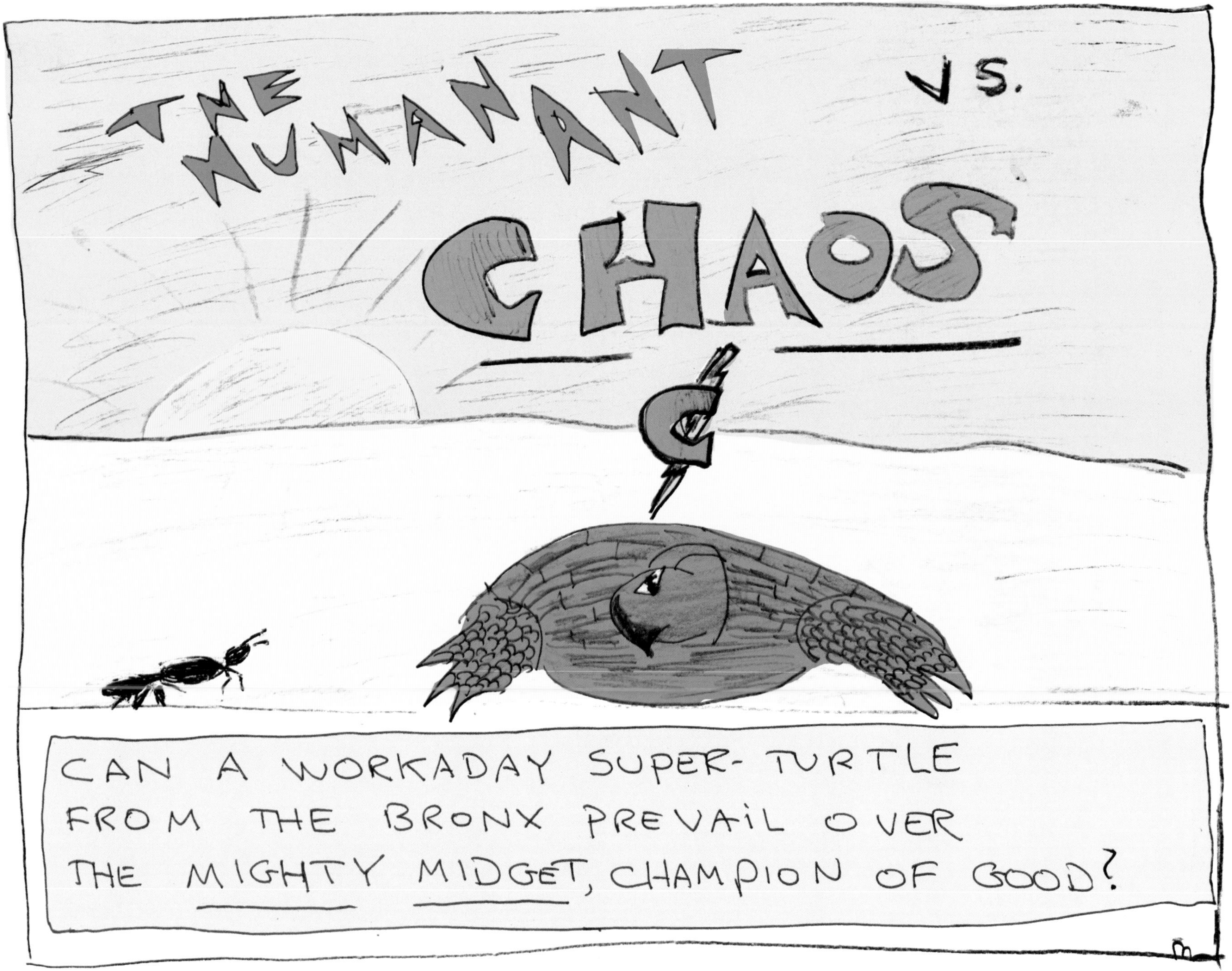
THE HUMANANT VS.
CHAOS
CAN A WORKADAY SUPER-TURTLE FROM THE BRONX PREVAIL OVER THE MIGHTY MIDGET, CHAMPION OF GOOD?

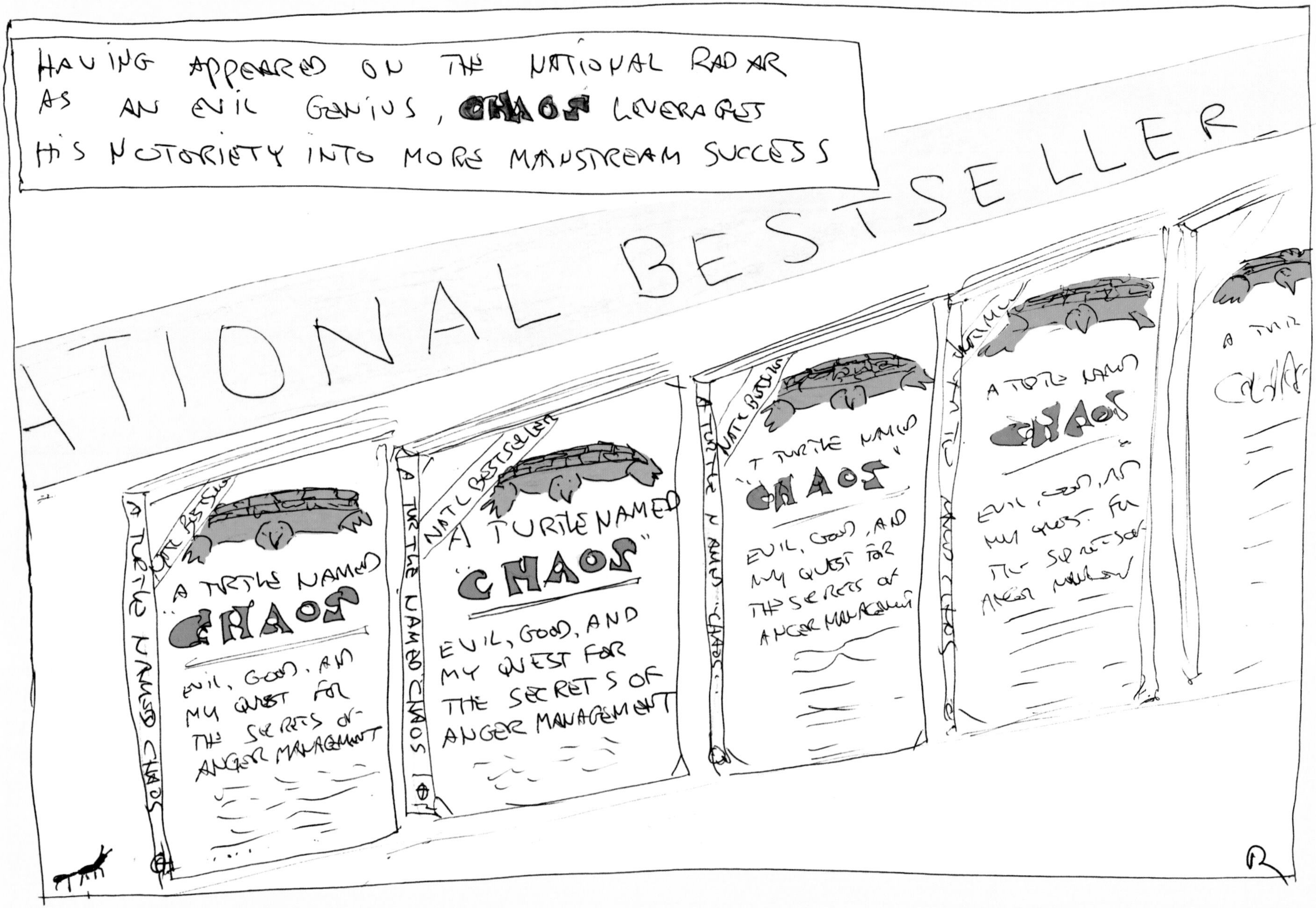
HAVING APPEARED ON THE NATIONAL RADAR AS AN EVIL GENIUS, CHAOS LEVERAGES HIS NOTORIETY INTO MORE MAINSTREAM SUCCESS
ATIONAL BESTSELLER
NAT'L BESTSELLER
A TURTLE NAMED "CHAOS"
EVIL, GOOD, AND MY QUEST FOR THE SECRETS OF ANGER MANAGEMENT
A TURTLE NAMED CHAOS

IN THAT BITTERSWEET MOMENT KNOWN TO ALL PARENTS + TEACHERS, ~~THE HUMAN ANT~~ INFORMS HIS SIDEKICK AND PROTÉGÉ, COCKY COCKROACH, THAT THE TIME HAS COME TO "LEAVE THE NEST" AND STRIKE OUT ON HIS OWN. THE SEQUELAE:

PROTESTATIONS OF INADEQUACY AND PLEAS TO BE ALL-OWED TO CONTINUE IN HIS ROLE.

POUTING

DEMANDS FOR LEGAL REDRESS

THAT THE PARTY OF THE SECOND PART, THE PLAINTIFF COCKFORD COCKROACH, DEMANDS OF THE PARTY OF THE FIRST PART, "ANTMAN" ACKNOWLEDGEMENT THAT ALL ADVENTURES FOR WHICH HE HAS CLAIMED CREDIT ARE IN EFFECT, APPROP-RIATED FROM, AND ARE THE INTELLEC-TUAL PROPERTY OF "COCKY" ... COCK-ROAC... THAT...

SOCIALLY CONSCIOUS CARTOONING

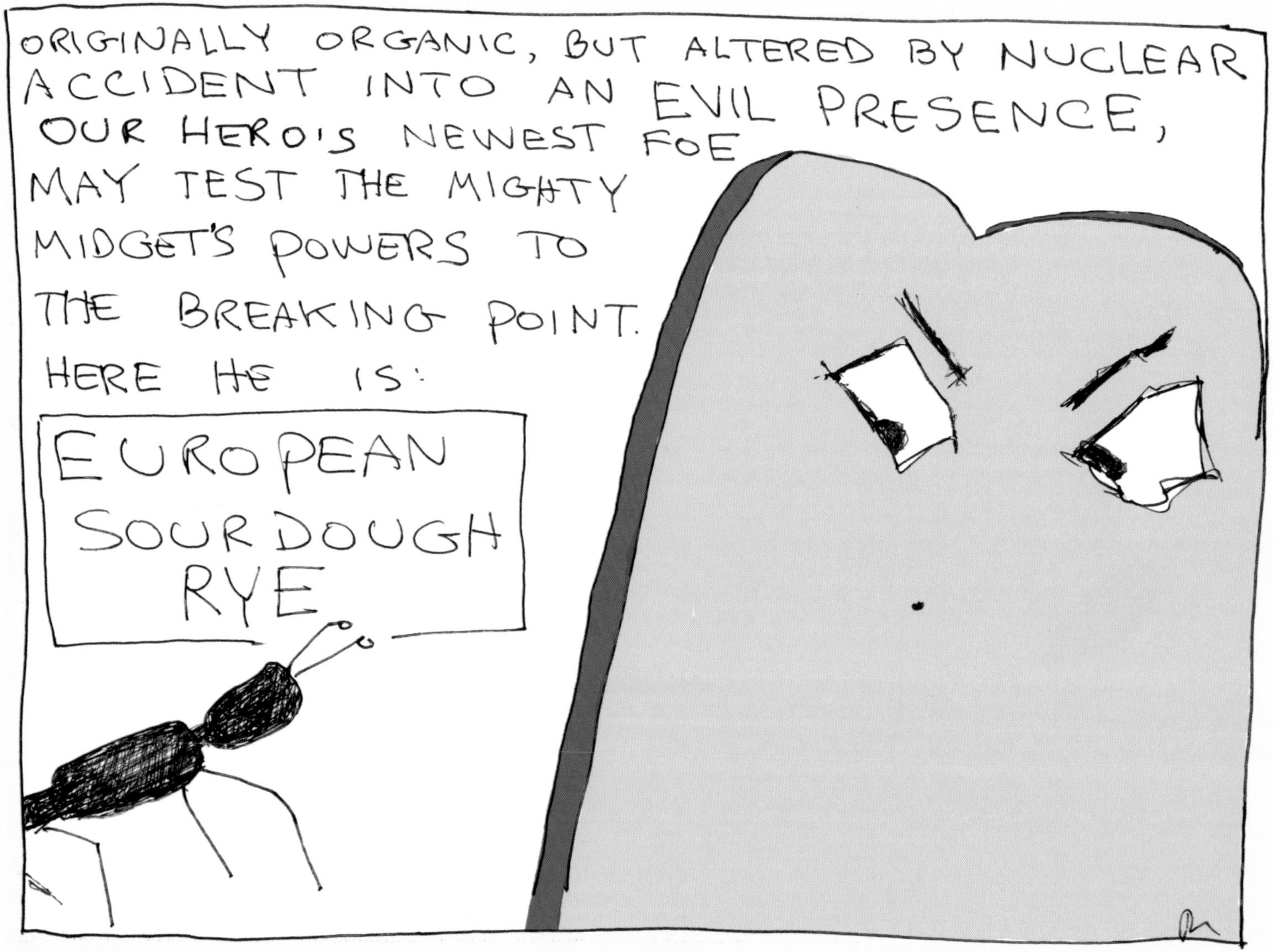

ORIGINALLY ORGANIC, BUT ALTERED BY NUCLEAR ACCIDENT INTO AN EVIL PRESENCE, OUR HERO'S NEWEST FOE MAY TEST THE MIGHTY MIDGET'S POWERS TO THE BREAKING POINT. HERE HE IS:
EUROPEAN SOURDOUGH RYE

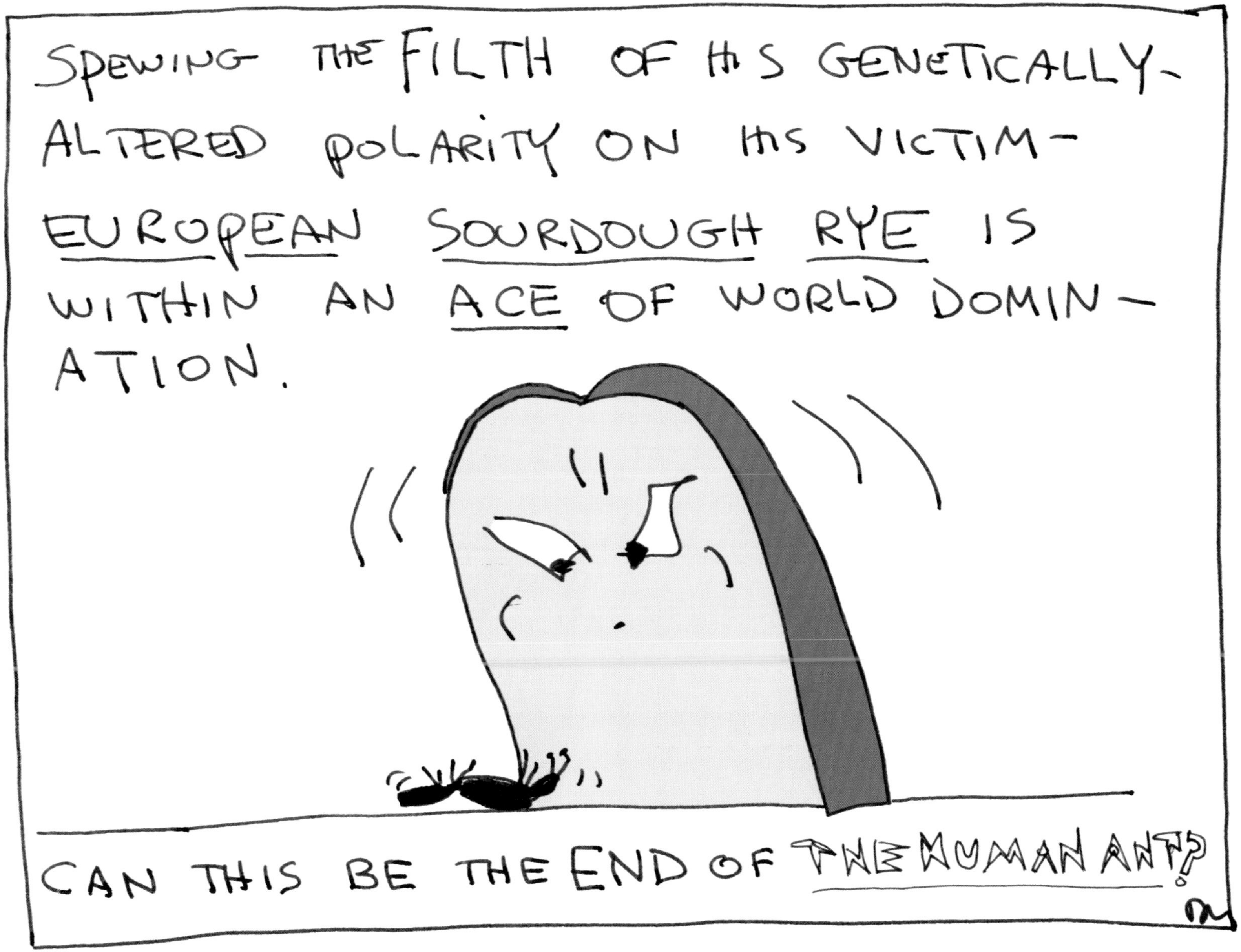
SPEWING THE FILTH OF HIS GENETICALLY-ALTERED POLARITY ON HIS VICTIM-EUROPEAN SOURDOUGH RYE IS WITHIN AN ACE OF WORLD DOMINATION.
CAN THIS BE THE END OF THE HUMAN ANT?

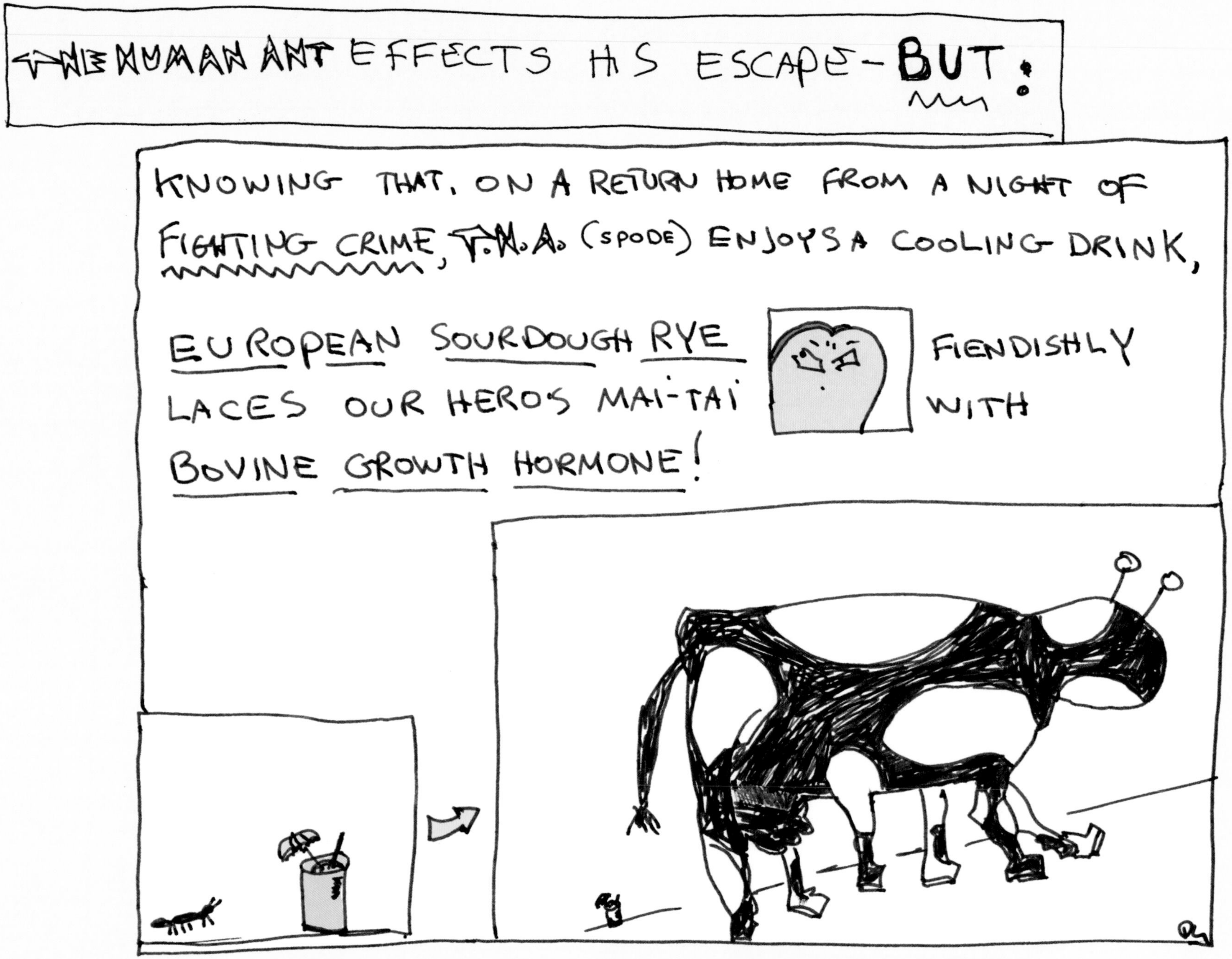
THE HUMAN ANT EFFECTS HIS ESCAPE—BUT:
KNOWING THAT, ON A RETURN HOME FROM A NIGHT OF FIGHTING CRIME, T.H.A. (SPODE) ENJOYS A COOLING DRINK,
EUROPEAN SOURDOUGH RYE FIENDISHLY LACES OUR HERO'S MAI-TAI WITH BOVINE GROWTH HORMONE!

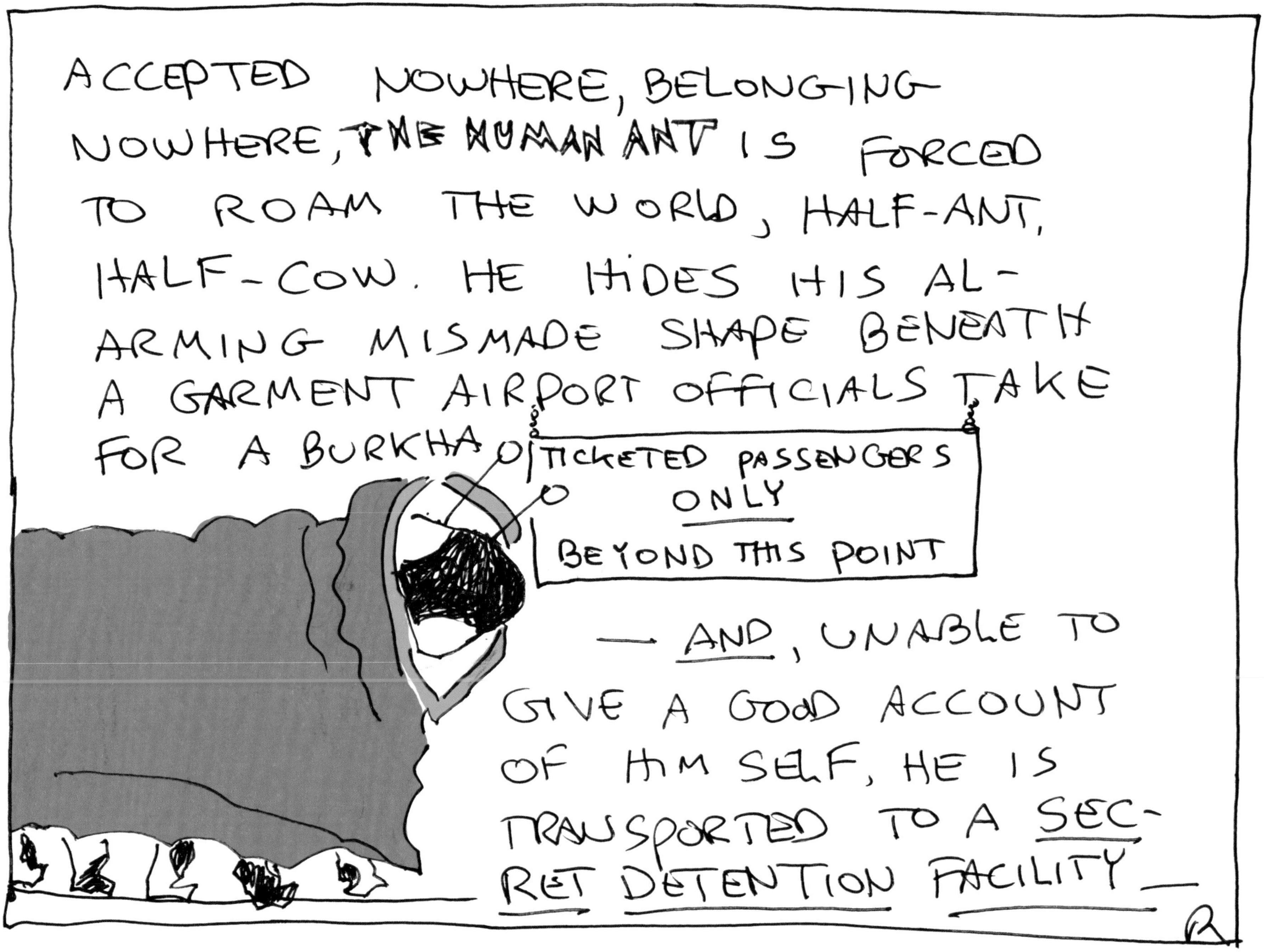
ACCEPTED NOWHERE, BELONGING NOWHERE, THE HUMAN ANT IS FORCED TO ROAM THE WORLD, HALF-ANT, HALF-COW. HE HIDES HIS AL-ARMING MISMADE SHAPE BENEATH A GARMENT AIRPORT OFFICIALS TAKE FOR A BURKHA
TICKETED PASSENGERS ONLY BEYOND THIS POINT
— AND, UNABLE TO GIVE A GOOD ACCOUNT OF HIM SELF, HE IS TRANSPORTED TO A SEC-RET DETENTION FACILITY —
R

WHILE INCARCERATED, HOWEVER, THE
EFFECT OF THE <u>BOVINE GROWTH
HORMONE</u> WEARS OFF, AND SPODE,
RETURNED TO HIS "TRUE" STATE, MAKES
HIS ESCAPE

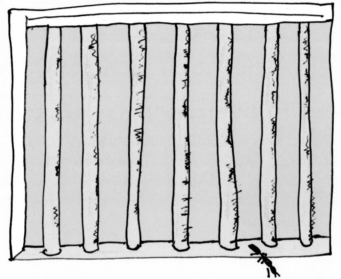

FAME

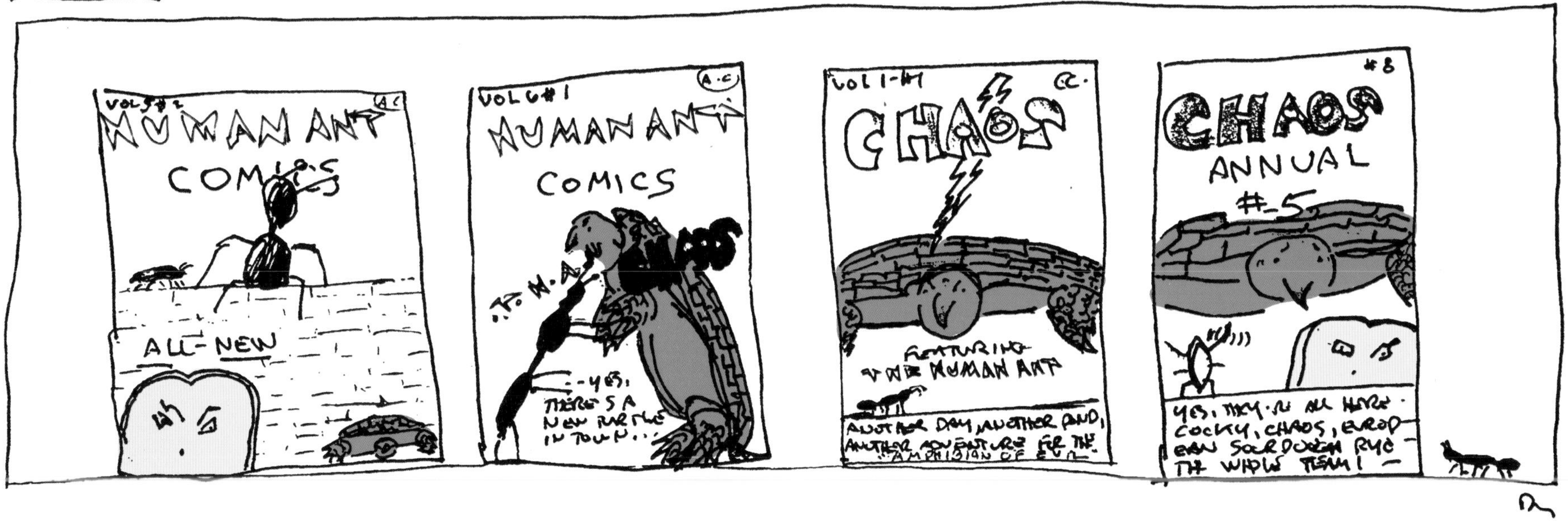

HUMAN ANT
COMICS
ALL-NEW
VOL 6 #1
HUMAN ANT
COMICS
CHAOS
--YES:
THERE'S A
NEW TURTLE
IN TOWN...
VOL 1-#1
CHAOS
#8
CHAOS
ANNUAL
#5

IT IS, HOWEVER, AN ILL-WIND THAT BLOWS NOBODY GOOD, AND, THE RAYS OF GENETIC-ALLY ALTERED POLARITY <u>WEAKEN THE SYSTEM</u> TO THAT POINT AT WHICH OUR HERO'S ORIGINAL, <u>GOD-GIVEN</u> <u>D.N.A</u> IS ALLOWED TO RE-ASSERT ITSELF

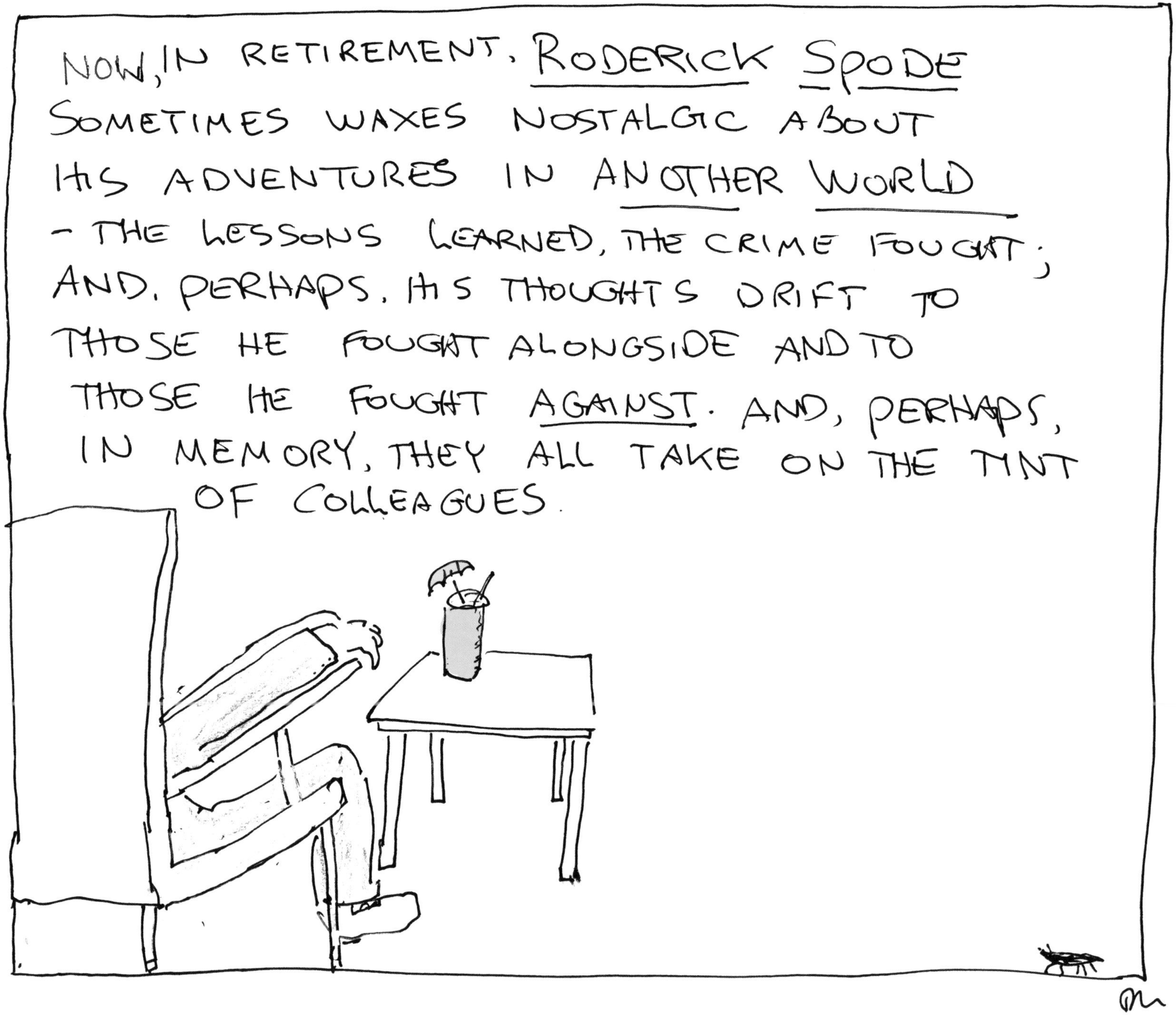
NOW, IN RETIREMENT, RODERICK SPODE SOMETIMES WAXES NOSTALGIC ABOUT HIS ADVENTURES IN ANOTHER WORLD - THE LESSONS LEARNED, THE CRIME FOUGHT; AND, PERHAPS, HIS THOUGHTS DRIFT TO THOSE HE FOUGHT ALONGSIDE AND TO THOSE HE FOUGHT AGAINST. AND, PERHAPS, IN MEMORY, THEY ALL TAKE ON THE TINT OF COLLEAGUES.

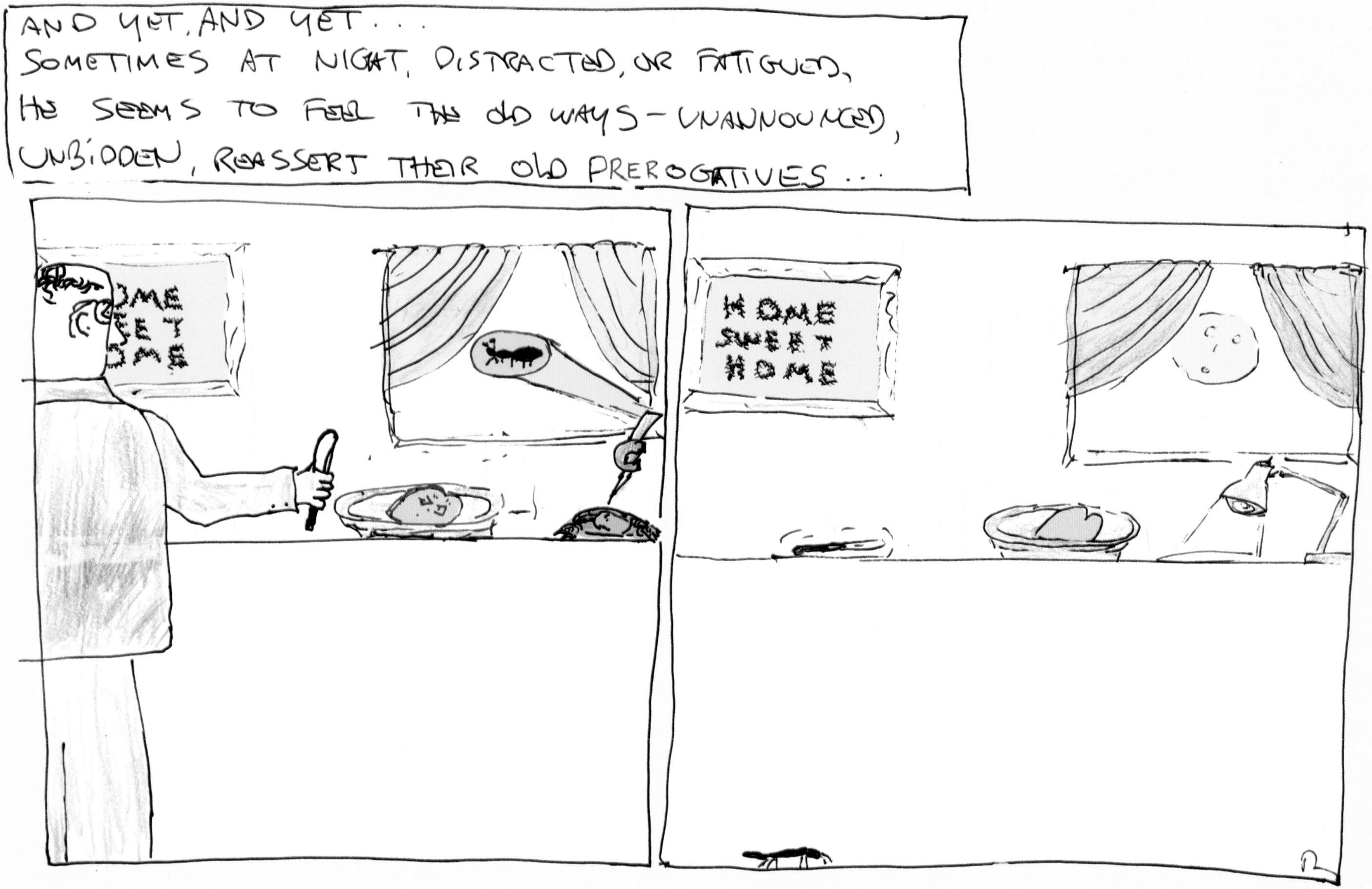
AND YET, AND YET . . .
SOMETIMES AT NIGHT, DISTRACTED, OR FATIGUED,
HE SEEMS TO FEEL THE OLD WAYS — UNANNOUNCED,
UNBIDDEN, REASSERT THEIR OLD PREROGATIVES . . .
HOME SWEET HOME

Nether regions of the earth-debarred,

O, self-conceited man, to thee,

The Trials of
Roderick Spode
The Human
Ant

Ants stride at will.

Humility is all.